Motorhome Maintenance
DIY and Save

By James Edward Clicquennoi

Dedicated to My Wife who has put up with my RV hobby for the past thirty-four years and supported me when I made the huge leap into a motorhome.

Read my other books

"RV TWEAKS MODIFICATIONS and UPGRADES Volume II"

"My Best RV DIY Projects"

available at www.Amazon.com.

Table of Contents

INTRODUCTION

Traveling with my parents when younger and then my own family I have been RVing for over 60 years. Between my father and I we have owned 9 different types of RVs from simple pop-ups, to travel trailers, and finally a diesel pusher motorhome. In all that time we have never taken our RV to anyone for repairs or service but done the work ourselves.

Over the years I have been asked how to maintain chassis components, body components and appliances in a motorhome. By doing many of these tasks yourself you can save some serious cash. I figure that in the past ten years I have easily saved myself $5.000. The tasks are not hard once they are understood.

I finally sat down and put this information into one book. This book is laid out so that you can read the entire text front to back or use it as a reference guide selecting one section and read what is required when performing that task. In most cases I have included parts lists and links where material can be found. I hope you find the information useful.

Oil Change in a Diesel Pusher

Every year I am asked what it takes to change the oil in a diesel pusher motorhome. The answer is either take you coach to a diesel mechanic and pay $300 to $500 or do the job yourself for under $100.

If you change your own oil in the family car you can do it in your diesel motorhome. Even if you do not change the oil in the family car you can still do the job in your diesel motorhome. You just need to be aware that everything is BIGGER.

The first step is to check your engine's owner manual to learn what type of oil to use and the proper oil filter. My coach has a Cummins 340 horse power IBs engine. My manual specified Valvoline Premiun Blue SAE 15W40 diesel motor oil with CES20081 or CJ-4/LS rating. You can find the rating on the motor oil container. It further specifies that I will need 15 quarts of oil if just draining the pan or 17.6 quarts if changing the oil and oil filter. My engine requires a Fleetguard LF 3970 oil filter which cross references to a Fram PH 8942 oil filter, easier to find in an auto parts store.

I have found if you watch the sales circulars at your local auto parts store the oil is usually on sale during the month of August for about $15.00 per gallon, a savings of $3.00 per gallon off the standard price. If you buy the oil filter one at a time it will cost about $18.00 but if you buy a case of filters the price can get as low as $11.00 per filter. Remember you will be doing this job again.

I like to change my oil every fall so that I put my coach away with clean oil. Used diesel oil has acidic properties and it is better for the engine not to leave that in the over the winter.

As I said everything is bigger on a diesel so before beginning make sure you have a catch pan large enough for the quantity of oil in the engine.

On the oil pan you will find two drain plugs. The oil is changed from the plug on the bottom of the pan. Please use caution when draining the oil. Never get under your coach raised on its leveling jacks as these 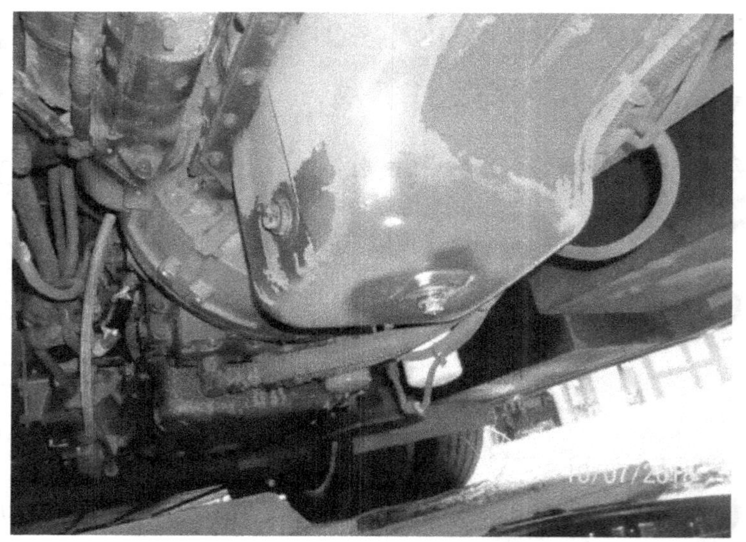 can fail and if the coach falls on you, goodbye. I recommend driving the back wheels of the coach up on 2 x 12 ramps. You may be fortunate enough to have a parking spot like I do where the back end of the coach extends over a depression in the ground, then no ramps are needed.

It is best to run the engine so that the oil is warm. Shut the engine off and using the proper size socket wrench remove the drain plug with the bucket placed under it. It may be necessary to hit the wrench to break the plug loose. Once the oil is drained reinstall the drain plug and snug.

Next you will want to change the oil filter. Mine can be found on the driver side of the engine. First, be sure that you can loosen it. I like to use a strap wrench with socket wrench and extension for this. I find this type of wrench can get into the tight confines around the filter.

Once loosened some people like to punch a hole in the bottom of the oil filter using a long flat blade screwdriver. This allows the oil to drain from the filter and filter housing and will prevent it running down your hand and arm. There is nothing worse than used diesel oil. It is dirty and black and will stain anything it touches.

Once removed, clean the oil filter housing with a clean rag. Take this opportunity to be sure the rubber O ring from the old oil filter has not stuck to the housing on the engine. Charge the new filter with fresh oil as this will prevent a dry start. Your engine will thank you. With your finger apply fresh oil to the rubber O ring on the filter and thread it on to the engine. Once snug you should turn the filter about ½ turn further by hand. DO NOT TIGHTEN WITH THE WRENCH.

Once the oil plug is back in and the new oil filter is installed it is time to refill the crank case with fresh oil. If lucky, the oil fill port will be in a convenient location. I have never been lucky. My fill port is above the radiator on the left side of the coach as I face the back of the

12

engine   Located at the top of the engine compartment the fresh oil bottle is too big to fit in the fill port. I have found a funnel will not work either. After many years I came up with the perfect solution. I saved a clean one gallon water bottle, pour the new oil into it and use this to pour oil into the engine. The water bottle is flexible enough to fit into the fill port.

Put in the proper amount of oil for your engine, Wait a few minutes for the oil to run down into the pan and check the level on the dip stick. Start the engine, let it run a few minutes, turn the engine off, and check around the filter and oil plug to assure no leaks.

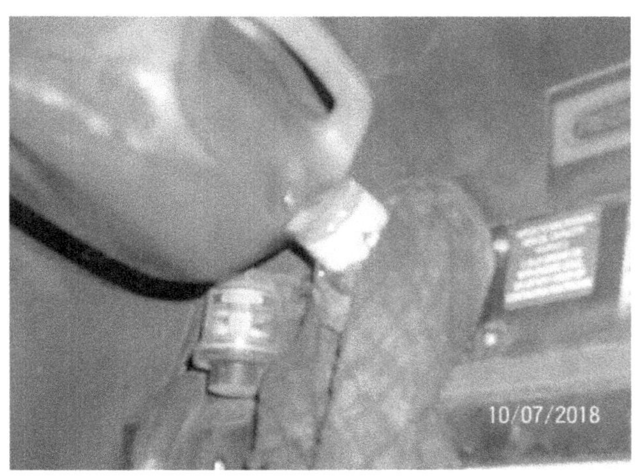

The last step is to dispose of the used oil properly. I pour it into the empty gallon jugs the new oil came in and take it to the auto store. They should have a recycle program.

Congratulations, you saved yourself several hundred dollars.

Once proficient you should be able to do an oil change in less than one hour. Your savings can be as much as $500 each time.

Generator Oil Change

In this section I am going to discuss the annual oil change and spark arrestor cleaning for Guardian 7.5K Quiet Diesel generator. The procedure is the same whether you have a Generac or Onan generator. At the end of the article I will have pictures for you Onan people.

I am one of the lucky few that have one of the last RV Generac Generators in my motorhome. What this means is that there is no one who will work on it when annual maintenance time comes along or when it breaks. You see, Generac got out of the RV generator business back in 2008 and all of their support facilities have disappeared. I have even called the company and the only support they could recommend to me was over 1000 miles from my home. That is a little far to go for the annual oil change. This has forced me to maintain and repair the generator myself.

 It is really not hard. My manual states that the oil and filter should be changed after every 150 hours of use or once a year, whichever occurs first. The manual also calls for one gallon of Rotella T5 10-30 diesel oil and Generac oil filter part number 0709390126 which crosses references to a Fram PH3682 oil filter. You should check your manual for the proper oil and filter to use.

Tools you will need are a socket set, oil filter wrench, bucket to drain the oil into, a funnel, flat blade screwdriver, and clean rags.

First, start and run the generator for a few minutes to warm up the oil. You can do this right at the generator as they all have controls on the unit as well as in the coach. To the right is a picture of the control panel on the Generac. You can  also see that the oil fill and dipstick are located in the same area. I switch off the circuit breaker so that I am not energizing the coach. This is not necessary, just something I do.

Once warmed up shut off the generator and remove the oil filler cap. This will allow the oil to run out more freely when draining. Next you will need to get under the generator. Caution, do not crawl under any motorhome that is up on its leveling jacks. I always run the front tires of my motorhome up on a 2 x 12 to gain access.

In every generator there will be an access door for service. On the Generac it is at the front. Remove the door and the air filter, fuel filter, oil filter and oil drain plug will be exposed. I need to remove the air filter to better expose the oil filter. This is not necessary for the Onan.

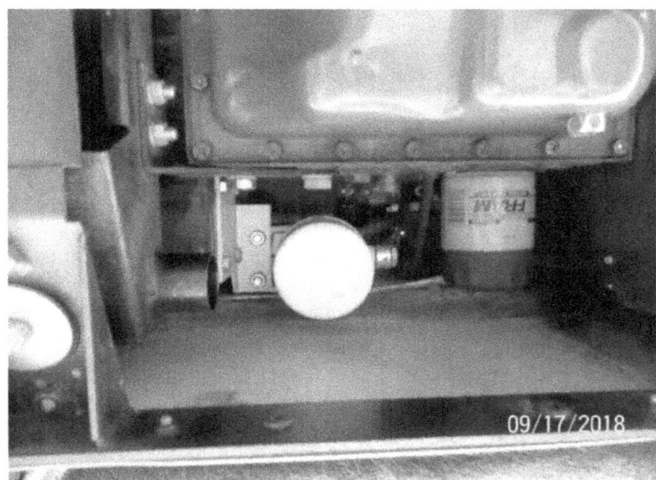

The oil plug is to the right of the oil pan and is clearly visible. I loosen this, then place the catch bucket under and remove the plug to drain the oil. Note here that used diesel oil is very black and will stain anything it touches. Have your rag available to clean up any spills. Once the oil has drained, replace the oil plug, then using the oil filter wrench remove the oil filter. Clean the area the oil filter attaches to making sure the old rubber O ring came off with the filter. Apply a coating of oil with your finger to the new oil

17

filter O ring and install on the generator. Hand tighten the filter then turn another ½ turn and no more or you will not be able to remove it next time.

Note as the oil filter is installed on its side I did not pre fill with oil. Fill the generator with the proper amount of oil and run for a few minutes. Check the filter and oil plug for leaks. Reinstall the access door.

On to the Spark Arrestor.

All generators are equipped with a spark arrestor so that the unit can be operated legally at U.S. Forest Service sites. The spark arrestor is a filter screen on the muffler that traps burning embers and soot that could start a grass fire. According to the service schedule the spark arrestor should be serviced at 250 hours or once each year. I normally do it at the time of the oil change. There will be a plug near the muffler. On my Generac it is labeled. Remove the plug and start the engine. The soot will blow out. At times I have needed to push a small screwdriver up the hole to loosen a carbon plug. Once the soot is cleaned out replace the plug, turn the circuit breaker back on and you are done.

Remember to dispose of your used oil properly. I normally pour it back into the empty oil container and return it to the auto parts store for recycling.

To follow are pictures of an 8K Onan RV generator drain plug, hatch where the oil filter is found and other important features.

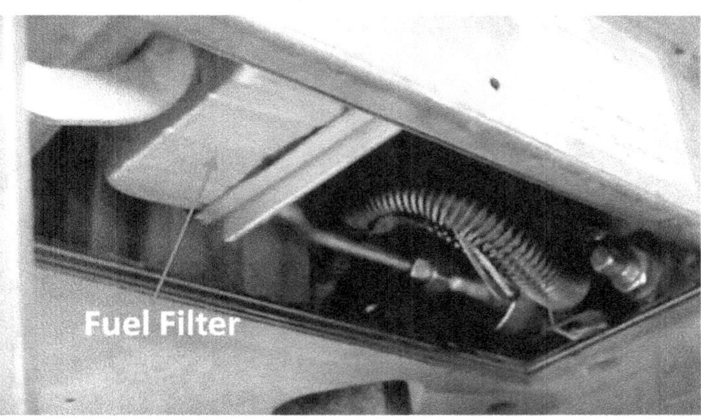

Exhaust pipe
Spark Arrestor Cleanout Plug

Spark Arrestor Plug Removed

Air Filter Housing

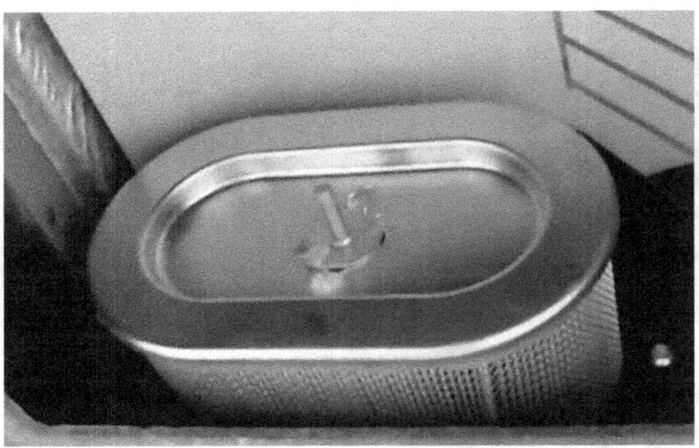

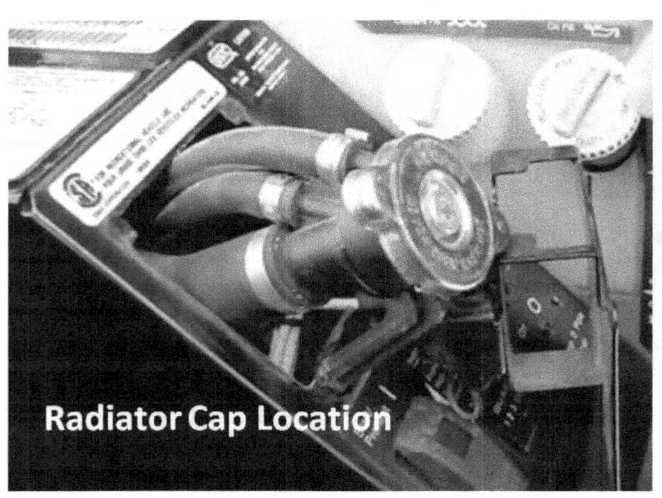

Radiator Cap Location

Coolant Drain On Bottom Of Generator

Fuel Filter Change

My coach is built on a 2007 Freightliner XC chassis and has a Cummins 6.7 liter ISB engine. The manual specifies that the fuel filter and fuel water separator should be changed every 15,000 miles.

Changing the filters is quite simple. First, check your manual to determine the proper part numbers. Mine are primary fuel filter Fleetguard number FF 5632 (cost about $20.00) and Fuel Water Separator Alliance part number ABP-N122 R50419 (cost about $40.00). The fuel water separator is actually an assembly consisting of the filter and a plastic bowl. The plastic bowl unscrews from the bottom of the filter and is reusable. I purchased an extra, just in case the original ever breaks. I believe the cost was $37. This was ten years ago and I purchased it from Freightliner at an FMCA show.

A little pricy for what you get but consider it insurance. Pictures below show the fuel water separator assembly.

At my initial filter change I found the fuel filter was stuck,

having been over tightened by the factory. I tried everything but could not get it free. Finally I found that a two foot channel lock pliers was the only tool that would loosen it. I was able to grip the filter around the reinforced neck and spin it off. Notice the filter comes with two rubber O rings. One is affixed to the filter and the second is to go around the screw shaft.

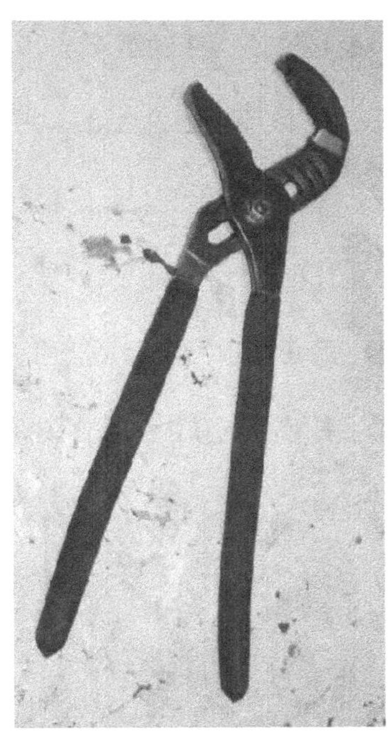

My filters are located on the passenger side of the coach next to the engine. They are easily accessible without having to raise the coach. I would suggest that the parking brake be set and the tires blocked to insure the coach will not move.

Start the coach prior to changing the filters. This is to insure it is working. If you cannot start the coach after the filter change you will know it was something you did and not another problem.

I got the following procedure when I was at Camp Freightliner, have followed it to the letter and have never had a problem.

- Have a bucket to catch any fuel that might spill. Some people have reported fuel leaking when the filters are removed. I have never experienced this.
- Do one filter at a time. This is to insure as little air as possible gets in the fuel system.
- Pre charge the fuel filter and fuel water separator with clean diesel fuel. Plug the center hole in the fuel filter and pour the fuel in the outside ring of holes. Pre charge will insure you do not have a dry start and vapor lock.
- Change the fuel water separator. Use the channel lock pliers or a strap wrench to loosen. Tighten by hand ½ turn beyond snug.
- Start the coach and immediately rev the engine to 2000 rpm until coach running smoothly. This is to bleed air out of the fuel system.
- Change the fuel filter. Use the channel lock pliers or a strap wrench to loosen. Tighten by hand ½ turn beyond snug.
- Again start the coach and immediately rev the engine to 2000 rpm until coach runs smoothly. This is to bleed air out of the fuel system.
- Check for leaks and you are done.

If you have problems starting the engine after the filter change use you may have gotten too much air in the fuel line. Turn your key to the on position five or six times but do not start the coach. Hold the on position for perhaps 20 seconds. On newer coaches the fuel pump will charge the filters and fuel lines.

Cummins ISB Air Filter Change

I often refer to the air filter on my diesel pusher as a big trash can. Why you may ask? Because it is as big as and looks like a small trash can. To the right is a picture of the air filter from a Cummins ISB 340 HP engine. The entire filter, case and inside element are disposable. On my engine the air filter part number is Freightliner part 114880-003, FRAM pare CA8130, or K&N part 38-2006S.

At my first filter change I went to the K&N filter. The reason for this was not the improved fuel mileage as K&N claims but for its robust construction. If you look at the air input opening in the picture you can see that the filter is enclosed in a wire cage. This is both on the air input side as well as the air output side of the filter. This wire cage was important to me because in every seminar I have attended the presenter would always tell a story of how a paper filter collapsed and got sucked into the air intake of the engine. This resulted in the need for an engine overhaul. These stories sufficiently scared me as to go the extra expense for the K&N filter.

I am happy to report that I have found an alternative to the K&N filter that is also built with an inner steal cage. This filter is manufactured by Parker Hannifin Corporation and is the same part number as the Freightliner filter, 114880-003. The instructions for this filter list the following change description:

- Improved corrosion resistance by upgrading the black painted carbon steel shell to a silver galvanized steel shell.
- Improved strength of the element by adding an inner steel shell.
- Improved seal of media, housing, and cage.
- Changed the filter adhesive from plastisol to a more environmentally friendly urethane.
- To learn more about this filter you can visit www.racornews.com.

The hardest part in changing the air filter is getting to it. On my coach this is done through the access hatch under the bed. Tools required are a screw driver and wrench and the task

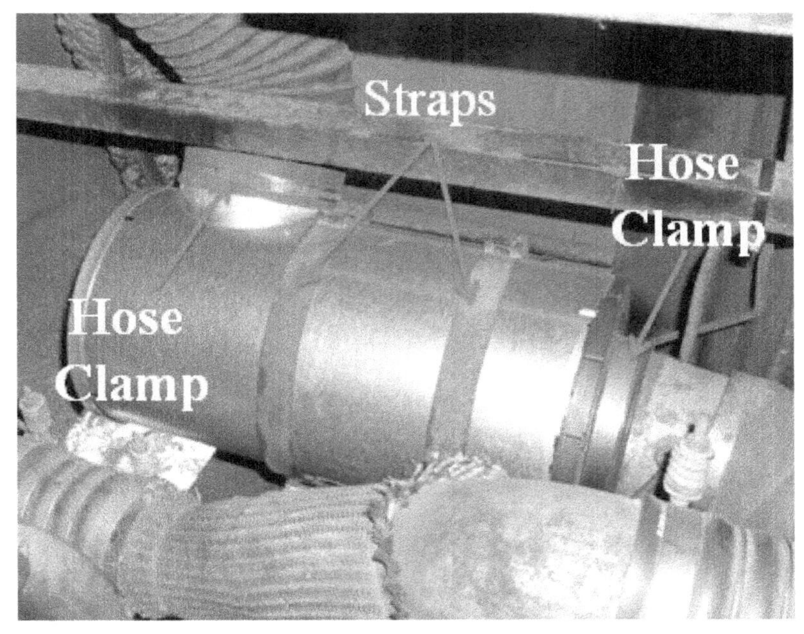

should not take over an hour.

Loosen the two hose clamps and remove the inlet and outlet tubing. Then unsnap the canister straps and remove the filter.

The new filter is installed in the reverse order. Caution, be sure not to get dirt in the outlet hose. Diesel engines are sensitive to breathing dirt.

When do you need to change the air filter? It should be changed annually or when the restrictor shows it is blocked which is when the yellow marker reaches the red change line.

When you have completed the filter change I would like to recommend you check the air inlet on the coach. Some are screened but some, like mine are not. I have heard many stories regarding birds making nests in these inlets. When you start the engine the nest is sucked into the air filter and you end up going nowhere. A simple solution to this is to attach a piece of rat wire to the inlet. I slide mine behind the fins and held it in with tie wraps.

Air Dryer Maintenance

If you run a Diesel Pusher then you have an air system on the coach comprised of a compressor, air tanks, air lines and an air dryer. This system is required for support of the air bag suspension and air brakes. An important part of the coach air system is the air dryer. The air dryer is designed to collect and remove contaminants in solid, liquid, and vapor form before they enter the air lines. Without a functioning air dryer these contaminants can cause your air system to fail and or freeze in cold weather.

My coach has a PURest Air Dryer manufactured by Haldex. The air dryer is located on the chassis frame, driver's side of the coach, just behind the rear wheels. The maintenance required for this system is to change the desiccant filter cartridge every three years. You can get a kit for this that contains everything required, the new filter, rubber O ring, and new bolts to reattach the cover. The kit cost is about $150.

Note: It is not recommended to use the old bolts or O ring when servicing this system.

 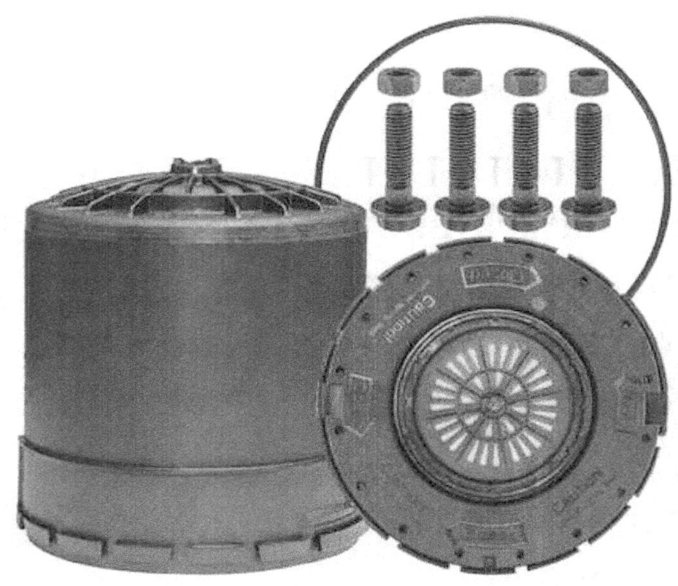

Some people actually remove the entire air dryer from the coach to service it but I have found that by running the rear wheels of the coach up on 2 x 12 ramps I am able to do the job with the dryer in place. Set the parking brake and chock the tires.

Please note when performing this task do not be tempted to crawl under the coach while it is raised on its jacking system. Should this fail and the coach fall you will not survive.

Tools required to change the desiccant filter are a socket set and clean rags.

First, bleed down the air system. This can be accomplished by pressing on the break peddle until the air gauges on the dash read zero and you no longer hear air hissing.

Now crawl under the coach and using your rags clean the unit. This will prevent dirt from getting in during the disassembly process. Remove the four 15 mm bolts that hold the cover in place. You will have to feel for the bolts. It can be done. I have changed mine three times with no issues.

Once the bolts are removed lift the cover off. This may take some persuasion. See pictures.

Press down on the filter and turn counter clockwise, it will come out of the cover. Clean the cover with your rags and install the new filter in the reverse order.   Insure the old rubber O ring has come off the air dryer body and install the new one.

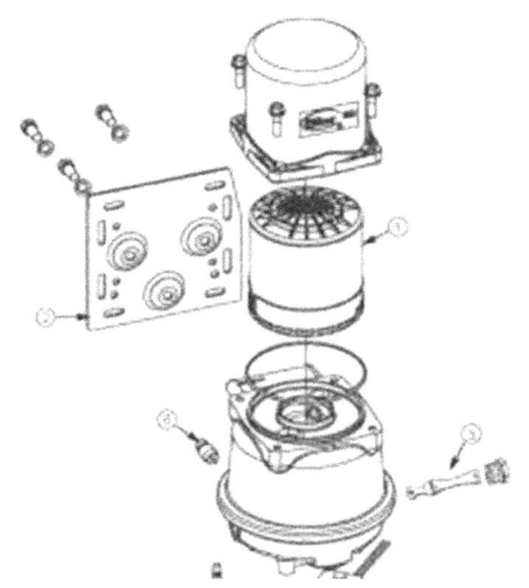

A little Vaseline will help it stay in place. Set the filter housing on the air dryer being careful not to distort the O ring and bolt down with the new bolts. Torque to 35 to 40 ft lbs. You should not have to force anything. If you do the O ring may have slipped.

Start the engine, and allow the air system to pump up. If it is taking longer than normal you may have a leak around the filter O ring.

It is good practice to go back and listen at the filter for any escaping air. If all is well you are done.

Maintain Front Wheel Bearings

One of the most overlooked areas of a diesel pusher
motorhome is the front wheel bearings. Unlike the family auto
that has sealed wheel bearings that you run until the wheels fall
off a diesel pusher motorhome has oil bathed wheel bearings
and they require maintaining.

For a Freightliner XC chassis the manual specifies that the oil
level should be checked at every engine oil change and the oil
changed every 24,000 miles or every two years whichever
comes first. Oil capacity is approximately 1 to 1-1/2 pints of
80W–90 hypoid gear oil in each hub.

Checking the level is easy. Remove the wheel or hub cap to
expose the hub. The hub cover is clear plastic and level can be
seen through the hub.

To change the wheel oil you will need a set of allen wrenches,
a funnel, catch cup, and wheel oil.

Move the motorhome so that the drain plug is facing down.
Remove the plug and catch the draining oil in the cup. As
wheel oil is thick it will take some time for it all to drain. Mine
took about ½ hour.

Once drained replace the drain plug, pull off the rubber fill cap and fill to line on the hub that indicates full.

Like draining, filling will take time for the oil to seep through the front bearings to the back ones so be patient.

The two pictures show the wheel hub with the drain plug and fill cap identified as well as the full line. The second picture is the wheel hub with the fill cap removed.

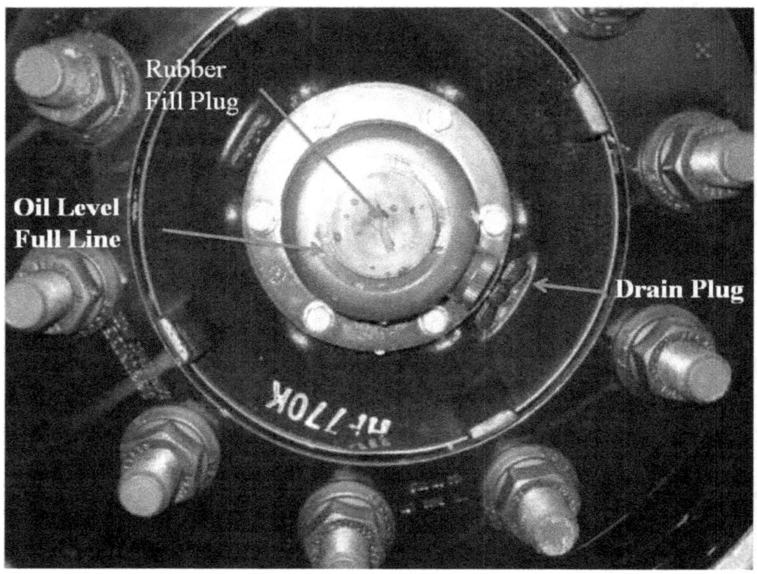

If you let your coach sit for any period of time, like through the winter, the wheel seals can develop flat spots and begin to leak. To check for this I look under the coach at the inside of the front wheel. If the wheel seal has gone bad you will see a streak of oil running down the wheel onto the tire and to the ground.

If you see this check the oil hub oil level, top off if needed, and have the seal replaced. The cost is about $200 at any diesel garage.

Driving on a dry bearing is not worth the risk and can result in a more costly repair.

Transmission Service

My coach has an Allison 2500 Transmission. There is not much to say regarding maintenance. Filled with Mobil DelVac SynTrans MBL 98Hx54 oil my manual specified an initial filter change at 3500 miles. I have read that later models are now specifying the first filter change at 10,000 miles. The transmission filter is external and looks much like an oil filter. To change this filter just spin it off, pre-charge the new filter and replace. The only transmission oil that will be lost is that which is in the filter. The 2500 uses an Allison part number 29539579 filter that cross references to a Fram P 9264 oil filter.

If filled with DelVac SynTrans oil the recommendation is to change the oil under normal driving after 120,000 miles. If driven under heavy duty loads it should be changed after 60,000 miles.

Since my coach has been driven in the mountains and for many short trips I choose to change the oil and filter at the 60,000 mile point. The capacity of the transmission is 16 quarts.

Tools required are a socket set, drain pan, and new filter. I can get to the drain plug and filter without raising the coach. The precautions I take are to set the parking brake, block the wheels, and be sure the engine is off.   Remove the drain plug from the transmission and catch the old oil, remove the old filter, reinstall the pan plug, transmission filter and refill with the proper oil. The transmission filter is on the bottom of the transmission near the fuel filters. When completed run the engine and check for leaks.

Grease Freightliner Chassis

My coach is built on a 2007 Freightliner XC chassis. The manual recommends greasing the chassis at every oil change. As the oil change is recommended every 15.000 miles or annually I have modified the greasing interval to every 10,000 miles. For me this is every other year.

Shooting grease into a fitting is not hard but getting to and finding the fittings can be. There are thirty grease fittings on my chassis. Just having that number dictates you have an automatic grease gun. Believe me given the number and location, you will not want to be pumping a manual gun.

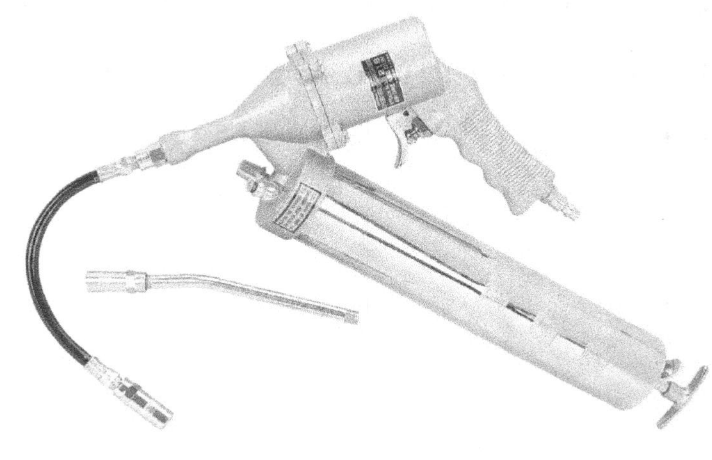

I purchased a pneumatic grease gun from Harbor Freight for under $20.00 and it has been worth every penny. You can also get battery grease guns but they are considerably more expensive. They may be the right option if you do not have a compressor

Crawling under the coach is going to require that you raise it up. I do not recommend crawling under while it is up on its leveling jacks. If they fail, you will be dead. I do the greasing in two sections, front then back. I run each section up on 2 x 12 ramps set the parking break and block the tires. Above all else be safe.

Below is information regarding where the grease fittings may be found. As there are so many I have tried to organize it in the manner that best helps me do the job. The hardest part is finding each fitting. Use a trouble light, it will help greatly. Once located wipe clean with a rag, connect the grease gun and pull the trigger. Some fittings will only require three or four trigger pulls. These are the ones with rubber boots around the joint. Do not pop the boot by over greasing. Fittings that require the grease to escape from the end of the joint will require more trigger pulls. See instructions in the tables.

Front of Chassis instructions.

Location	Comment	Number Of Fittings
Steering	Steering gear has one fitting. Steering shaft has three fittings. Drag Link & Bell Crank Two grease fittings per drag link; one on each end and one on bell crank housing.	9
Knuckle Pins	One on top and one on bottom	4
Slack Adjusters		2
Brake Camshaft Bracket	One grease fitting; Pump in grease until it appears at the slack adjuster end of the bracket	2
Tie Rod		2
Neway Independent Front Suspension	One on top & bottom of knuckle post	4
	Total number of fittings in front	**23**

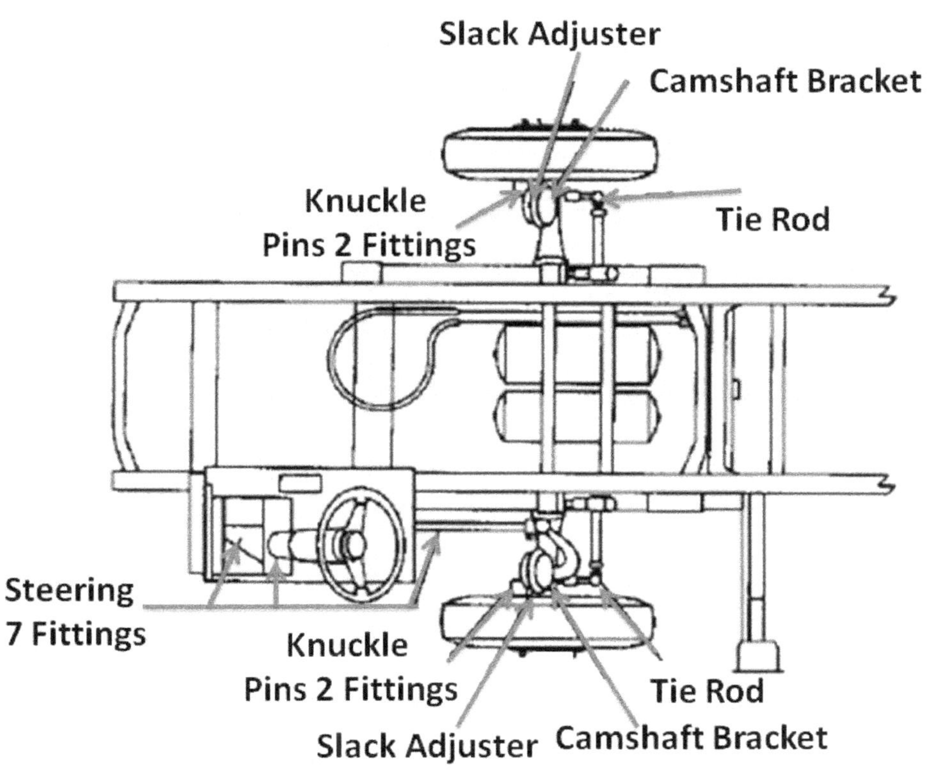

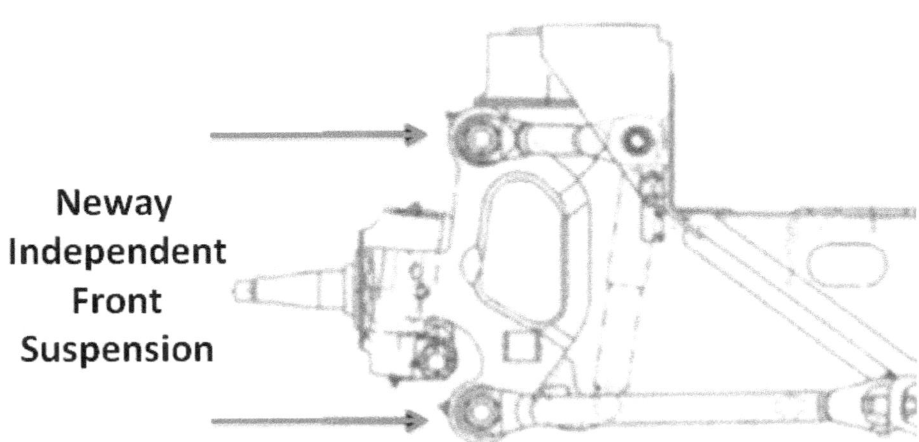

Kingpins you will grease until the grease comes out of the joint as specified in the table.

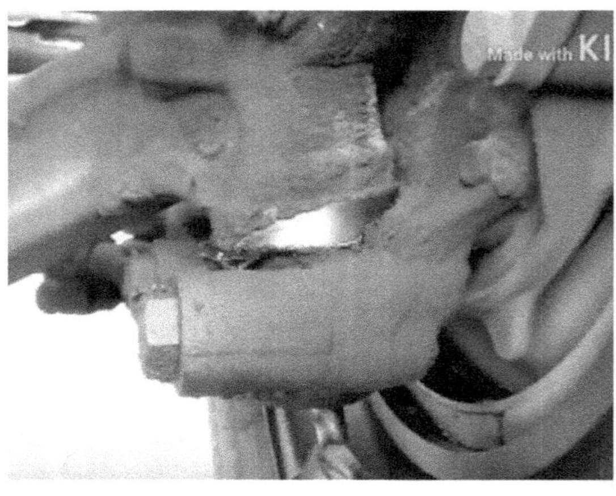 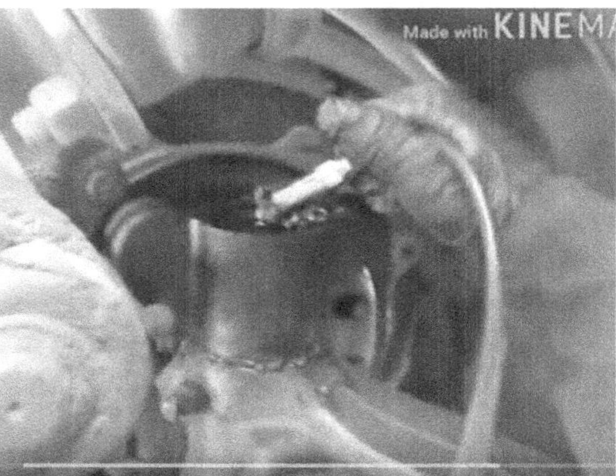

This is an example of what a rubber boot may look like.

Rear of Chassis instructions.

Location	Comment	Number Of Fittings
Slack Adjusters		2
Brake Camshaft Bracket	One grease fitting; Pump in grease until it appears at the slack adjuster end of the bracket	2
Driveshaft	Lubricate both universal joints & slip joint spline	3
	Total number of fittings in back	7

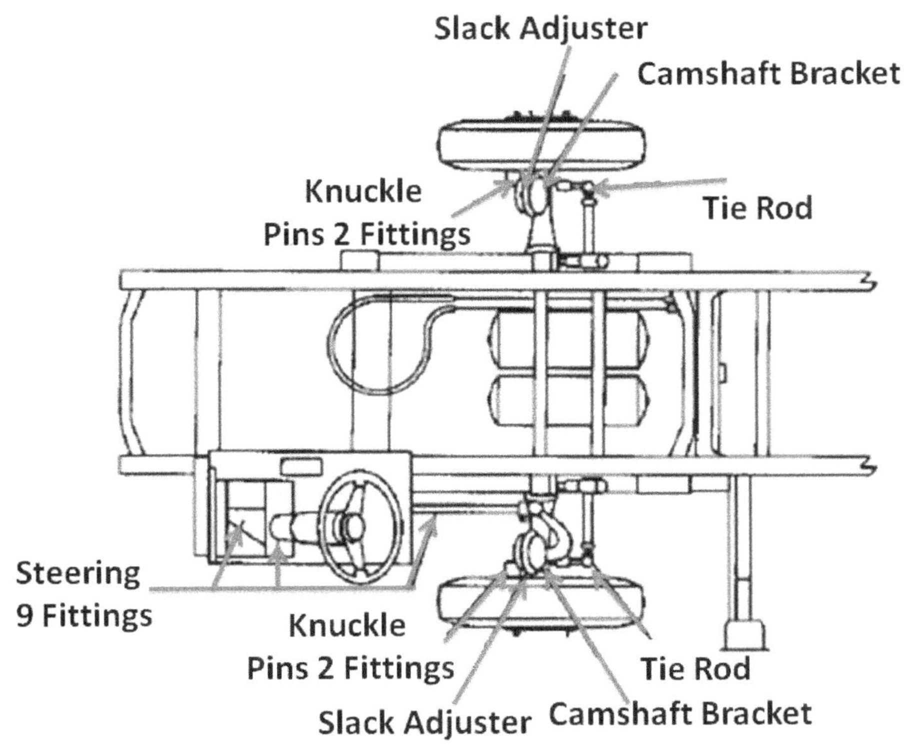

Locating the grease fittings may be difficult so I have included a picture.

Dash Airconditioning

During the summer months I constantly get the query "do you have any recommendation for my dash air conditioning? It no longer blows cold". What has probably happened is that the R134a coolent has leaked out of the system. This happens when the air conditioner is not used for a long period of time and the AC pump (located on the engine) seals dry out. The best fix for this is to get to the shop, have the system checked, and repaired as necessary. A stop gap for a shop visit and posibility a savior in the middle of a trip is to recharge the air conditioner your self. This is a very easy task and only takes a couple of minutes. Everything you need can be found at Walmart or your local auto parts store.

I like the product A/C PRO with stop leak. While a little pricey at $32.00 for a 16 oz can with gauge it is mixed with an AC stop leak formula that helps to recondition the seals. It has a reusable hose system with gauge and the gauge allows you to compensate for ambiant temperature. The directions on the can are clear and accurate.

If you look in the engine compartment of the coach you will find the condenser and blower box. Normally somewhere around them is a tag specifying the amount of R134a required for your system. My coach takes 3.4 pounds. Never put more than that into the system as you can cause further damage to seals and make the leaks worse.

One can of A/C PRO is 16 oz or one pound of R134a. If necessary suplement this with store brand R134a that comes in 12 oz cans for a more reasonable price of $5.00.

So you have purchased A/C PRO and a couple of cans of supplemental R134a. Now it is time to charge the system. You will need the engine running, the dash air conditioner turned on with the fan on full and the temperature setting at maximum cold.

The AC system will have two access ports. One on the high pressure side and one on the low pressure side of the system. We will be working with the low pressure port. How do I know which is which you ask? The two ports are different sizes. The AC Pro hose will only fit on the low pressure port. You cannot get it wrong. You are going to find the low pressure port at the front of the coach on the line leading to the condenser.

 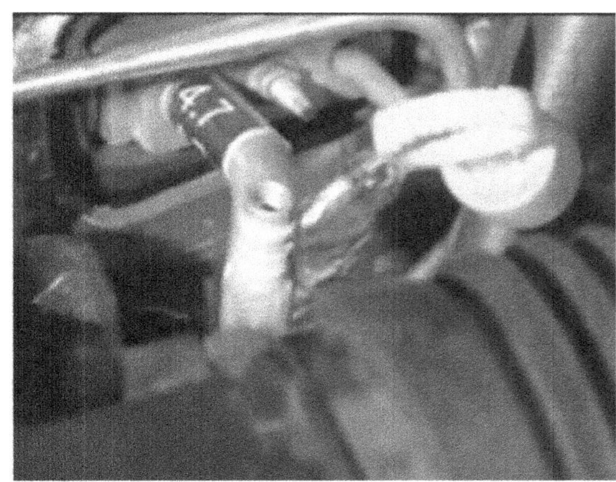

 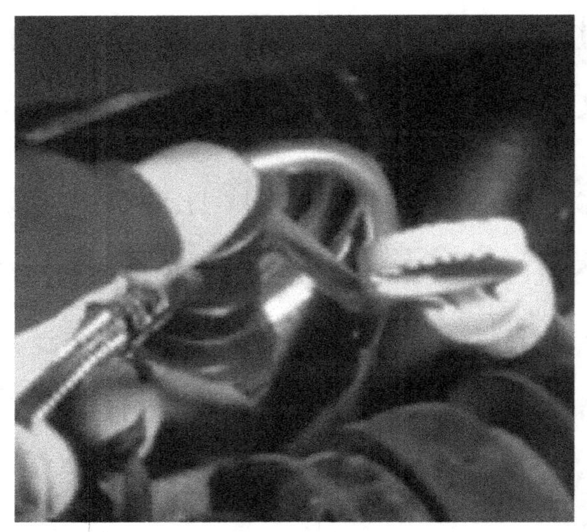

Remove the cap from the low pressure port, attach the AC Pro hose, set the air temperature on the gauge as directed to by the directions, and with the can upside down pull the trigger. Congratulations you are charging the air conditioner. Shake the can while charging and periodically stop and check the pressure reading. When the gauge reads into the green stop. Upon exhausting the first can move the gauge and hose to a new can and continue. Be careful when changing the gauge to a new can of R134a as the cans are under pressure. Keep the opening pointed away from your body in the event any gas escapes. Never put more R134a into the system than it is designed for no matter what the gauge reading and if there is gas left in the last can just leave the gauge and hose attached. It will keep until the next use.

When complete, put the cap back in the port and save the gauge and hose. In the future you can purchase just the AC PRO without it and save some cash.

You can measure your success as the temperature of air coming out of the dash vents should be 20 degrees below the outside air temperature.

I recommend that at some point you get the air conditioning system checked out by a certified mechanic and correct whatever caused the leak.

Dash Vents Do Not Blow Air

This is more an informational note. This past summer there have been a lot of motorhome owners complaining they are not getting any air out of their dash vents. They spend countless hours chasing down nonexistent fuses and/or wiring errors when it has been a failed vacuum pump. That is right, I said vacuum pump. In the automotive industry the vents are controlled by vacuum. Cars often tap this from the intake manifold on the engine while trucks and yes motorhomes have a special pump. Where has the body builder hidden it? Who knows. You will have to search under the dash, on the fire wall or in the electrical cupboard. The electrical cupboard is where mine is.

When you turn the key to the on position if you listen you can hear it turn on and pump up. I add this section only to perhaps save you hours of chasing ghosts if you lose your dash air. A new pump will run from $60.00 to $100.00.

I have Broken Down, Now What

Despite all your efforts sometimes break downs happen. Speaking from experience this never happens at a good tile like in our driveway or when you are parked. It normally happens while on the road. You are driving along, not a care in the world and THEN! The coach begins to beep.   You look down at the dash and see the dreaded RED IDIOT LIGHTS. You now have perhaps 10 seconds before the engine control

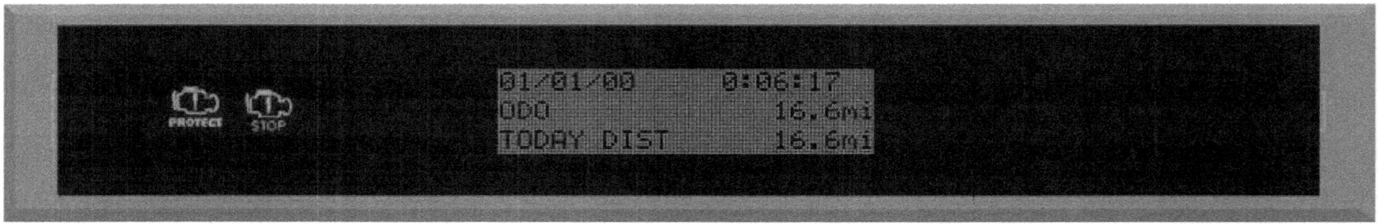

computer in its fare wiser wisdom shuts down the engine and leaves you stranded. After you acknowledge that sick feeling in the pit of our stomach you make a frantic effort to get to the side of the road and often coast to a stop. Our copilot adds to the confusion by exclaiming WHAT THE H$#& ARE YOU DOING!

I hope at this point you had the for sight to sign up for a road side service plan and or a tow plan because if a wrecker is required, one that can handle a motorhome the cost will be north of $1000.

There are several plans available. I am not going to make a recommendation but I will list them. I also want to add that if you did not have the for sight to purchase a plan Coach-Net is the only one I know of that will let you sign up for their plan and call them five minutes later and report a breakdown and need for a tow. Don't ask me how I know this.

To follow are available plans. I am sure there are more. These are the popular ones. The cost is usually less than $100 per year. Think of it as insurance you should not be without.

- Some insurance companies have plans. You would need to query yours.
- AAA. This differs by location. My AAA in MA does not offer a plan for RVs but I have friends in Ohio that swear by theirs.
- Coach-Net 1-800-601-2850
- Good Sam 1-800-601-2850
- FMCA 877- 581-8581

You have explained to your copilot what is going on and it is time to call your emergency service provider. First always tell them you are not in a safe location unless you want to holiday where you are. Next here is a list of useful info to have available. I have this info in my emergency package. I will show you the list with my info entered. I need to add if you specify the repair location and they will not work on the coach the Road side assistance service will NOT tow you again. If they specify the repair facility and the same happened they will come back and move you to another. I learned this the hard way.

Towing Method	Tire Lift Mechanism
Motorhome Make & Model	Forest River Berkshire VIN
Chassie Make and Model	Freightliner Raised Rail (800-385-4357)
Vehicle Length	40 Feet
Total Vehicle Weight Rating	33,000 Pounds
Front Axle Weight	10,500 Pounds
Rear Axle Weight	17,500 Pounds
Distance Between Front Bumper and Center of Steering Axle	7 Feet
Front Axle type	I-beam suspension w/ bell crank
Vehicle Height	12 1/2 feet
Type of Suspension	Air Ride
Generator Location	Front
Transmission Make and Model	Allison 2500
Transmission Type	Automatic
Cell Phone Number	978-761-5625
Location	

Questions

Name person Speaking to & Call Back Number	
Fees & Cost for Towing	
Additional cost to remove Driveshaft or Halfshaft (seal halfshaft openings)	
Paint Protection Against Cable Rub (towels).	

The following are a list of phone numbers that may be useful.

IMPORTANT SERVICE NUM-BERS	
Freightliner 24/7 Help Line	(800) FTL-HELP
Freightliner Chassis Corporation	(800) 385-4357
Freightliner Service Center, Gaffney, SC	(864) 206-8613
Caterpillar Engine Support	(800) 447-4986
Cummins Engine Support	(800) 343-7357
Allison Transmission	(800) 524-2303
Michelin Tire	(800) 847-3435
Mercedes Engine Support	(313) 592-4268
Dometic Corporation	(800) 544-4881
Norcold Corporation	(800) 543-1219
Onan Generator	(800) 888-6626
Aqua-Hot Heating	(800) 685-4398
Shurflo	(800) 762-8094
Tiffin Motorhomes Parts/Service	(256) 356-0261

OK, the coach has been towed and you are finally at the repair facility, hopefully the same day but nit often. In my emergency kit pack I have pre printed instructions for the shop. When you see them you will probably think I suffer from OCD but after seeing a mechanic take a pry bar to my coach because he did not know how something worked I put these together. I always keep several printed sets in the coach. After a slight chuckle I normally get a thank you for this info.

Clicquennoi Berkshire Keys

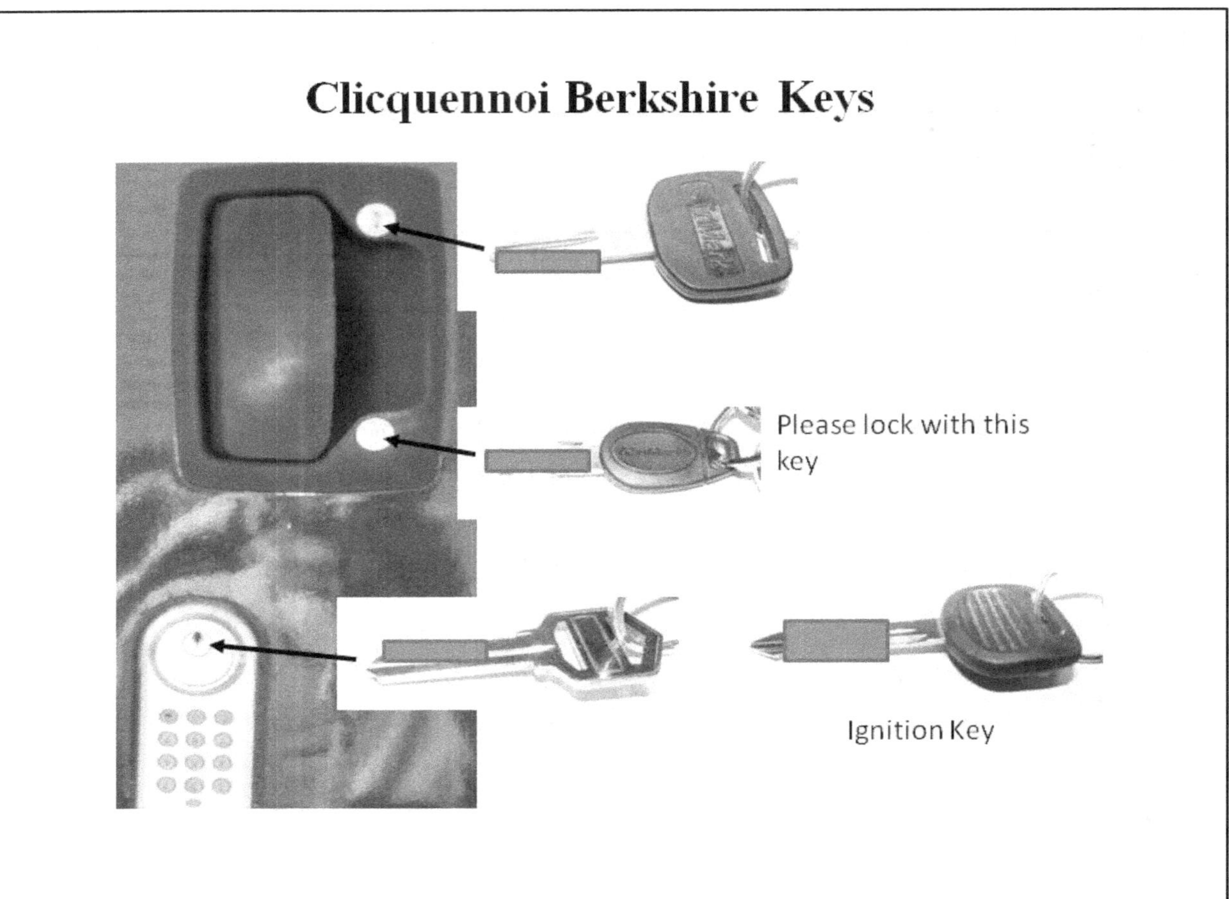

Clicquennoi Berkshire Battery Disconnect

Battery Disconnect

Just inside the door in the stare well on the right is a battery disconnect switch. To save the battery please press the switch when not using the coach.

Thanks

Clicquennoi Berkshire Inside Engine Access

Engine Access is under rear bed. Rear slides can be moved from control panel found passenger side mid coach then bed can be raised. There is a prop under the bed to hold it up.

Rear slide control switches

Passenger back side

Drivers back side

Clicquennoi Berkshire Electrical Bay Driver's Side

Generator Release

Clicquennoi Berkshire Wheel Simulator Removal

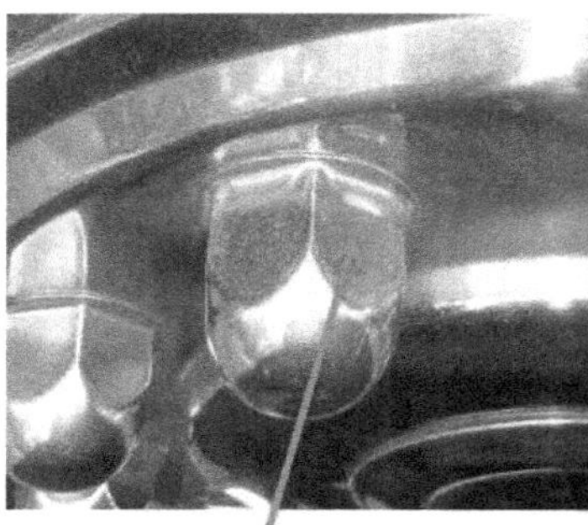

Wheel Simulators are held on by two nuts on each wheel. The nuts can be identified by a dimple. They are across from each other. When installing they should be hand tightened and not torque.

Do not use stabilizers to raise wheels off the ground. This will damage the stabilizers and may result in injury.

Clicquennoi Berkshire Battery Bay Passenger Side

Chassis Shutoff

Bay Key

Coach and
Generator Shutoff

Where Did My Hot Water Go?

Water heaters may look daunting but they are really very simple. Whether you have an Atwood or Suburban model, six gallon or ten gallon, gas only or gas and electric they all work about the same. There is a control board, safety fuse, and thermostat. For propane models there is the addition of a DSI circuit (Direct Spark Ignition), a gas valve with gas burner, and thermal burn out fuse. For electric models there is an on/off switch and electric burner or element.

Let's trouble shoot the gas water heater first.

- Some water heaters have circuit breakers. Have they tripped? Pressing them will verify.

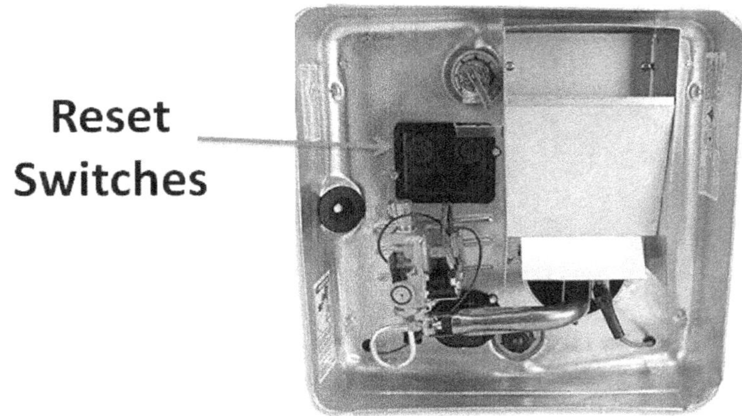

- Are all electrical connections good? Over time connections may oxidize. Check all including those on the circuit board and clean if necessary. Try to restart the water heater.

- Is there a bad fuse in the 12v circuit feeding the water heater or on the water heater circuit board? If yes, replace the fuse.

- Is it getting gas? A good way to test for gas is to light the stove. This accomplishes two things. It verifies the propane is flowing and purges the line of air. Visually check the burner for dirt. Insects called mud wasp can plug up the burner and their presence is easily seen. If there is one, use a small brush or compressed air to remove it. Try to restart the water heater.

- Is the DSI working? When turned on the DSI should make a clicking noise. There will be three ignition cycles or clicking cycles and if the unit fails to 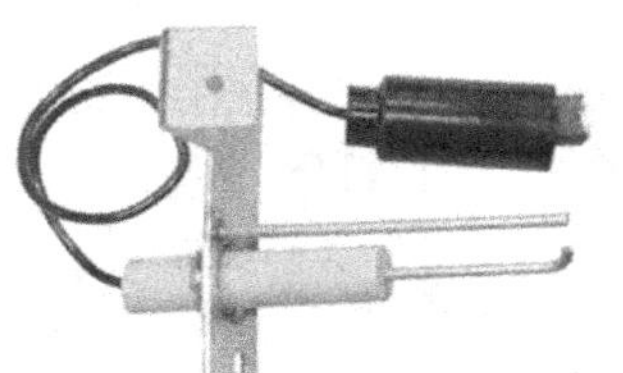 light, the DSI will go into lock-out mode. To come out of lockout turn the gas side of the water heater off then on. To verify if the DSI is bad or the circuit card feeding it unplug the device from the circuit card. Have someone turn on the gas water heater while you hold the positive probe of your ohm meter to the circuit card connection point and the negative probe to ground. If you do not see a voltage the printed circuit board is bad and must be replaced.

- Is the thermostat or emergency cut off device good? When the water heater is cold these should show short if tested with an ohm meter. Replace if bad.

- Is the thermal runaway fuse good? This device should look like a short if tested with an ohm meter. Replace if bad.

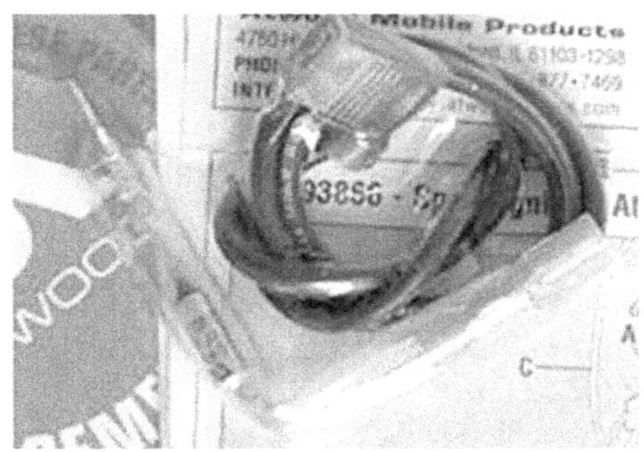

- If all the above check out then it is most likely a bad circuit board and it will need to be replaced.

When testing parts for continuity they should be isolated. Any of the parts discussed can be found at an RV supply store or on Amazon. Just be sure to purchase the correct ones for your brand and model water heater.

Let's trouble shoot the electric water heater.

- Again, some water heaters have circuit breakers. Have they tripped? Pressing them will verify.

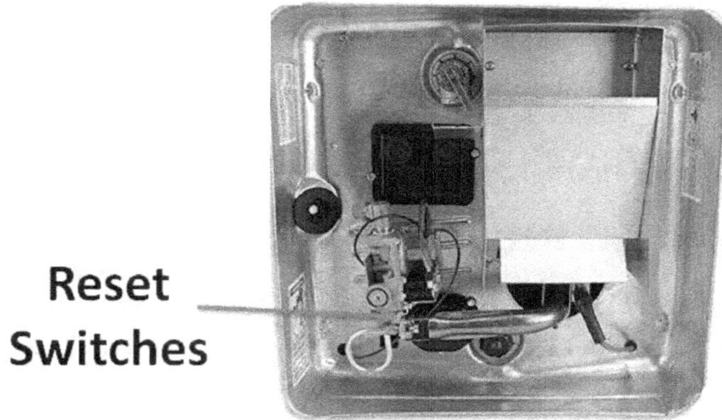

- Are all electrical connections good? Over time connections may oxidize. Check all including those on the circuit board and clean if necessary. Try to restart the water heater.
- Is there a bad fuse in the 12v circuit feeding the water heater or on the water heater circuit board? Is the AC circuit breaker off? Correct the issue and try again.
- Is the thermostat or emergency cut off device good? When the water heater is cold these should show short if tested with an ohm meter. Replace if bad.

- Is the heating element good?
  This should look like a low
  resistance if checked with a ohm
  meter. Turning on electric water heated with no water in it
  can blow the heating element in 5 seconds. If needed
  replacements can be obtained from Lowes for less than
  $20.00 while an RV store will want cost to $100.00.

- Is the on/off switch good? This may be inside
  the coach or behind the water cover outside. It
  can be pulled out, disconnected, and tested with
  a ohm meter. If bad replace.

- If all the above check out then it is
  most likely a bad circuit board
  and it will need to be replaced.

When testing parts for continuity they should be isolated. Any
of the parts discussed can be found at an RV supply store or on
Amazon. Just be sure to purchase the correct ones for your
brand and model water heater.

That is all there is to a tank type water heater.

Battery Care

Two things that are important to ensure the longevity of your coach batteries is to keep them watered and keep them charged. Let's talk about watering first.

Keeping my chassis batteries watered is easy as they are sealed. That done we move on to the coach batteries. My battery bank is made up of four six volt batteries configured into one twelve volt bank. These batteries are not sealed so I need to check the water level monthly. It is important to keep the plates covered but not to overfill the batteries or they will out gas.

For some time I have had my eye on a battery watering system. This past summer I purchased one and installed it. My configuration required two kits as well as the optional fill hose. My cost was $109.00. You may think this is a lot of money but as age and bad knees have caught up with me it has become more reasonable.

Each kit consists of six caps, tube system to connect the caps, red plugs for the unused ports and a length of hose. Also shown in the picture is the fill hose with rubber bulb. The first step in the installation is to

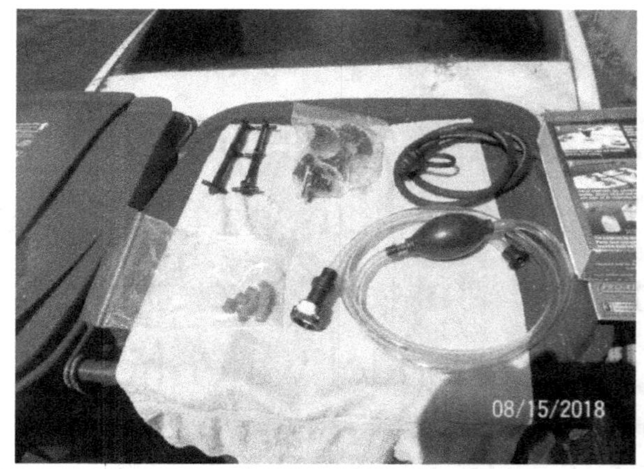

64

connect the caps to the batteries, next install the tube system to the caps. Note: press hard on the tubes so that they will seat into the caps. The final step is to interconnect the tubs system with the provided hose and water the batteries. Remember used distilled water.

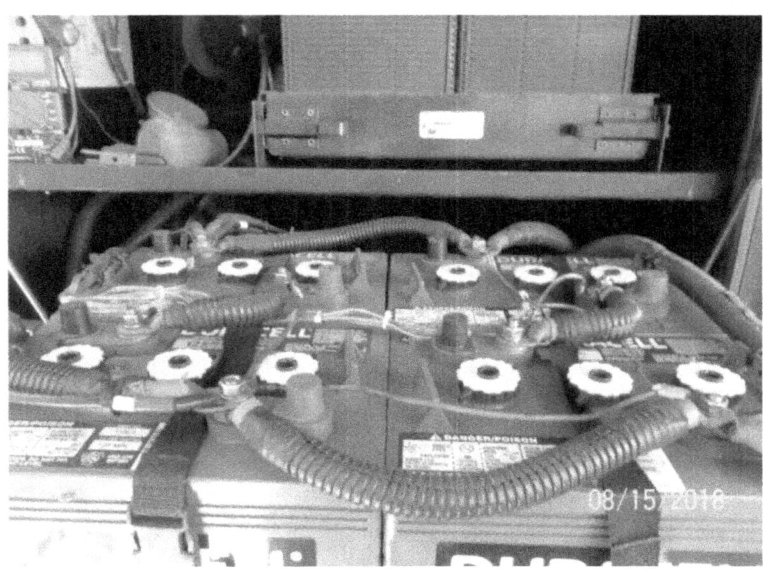

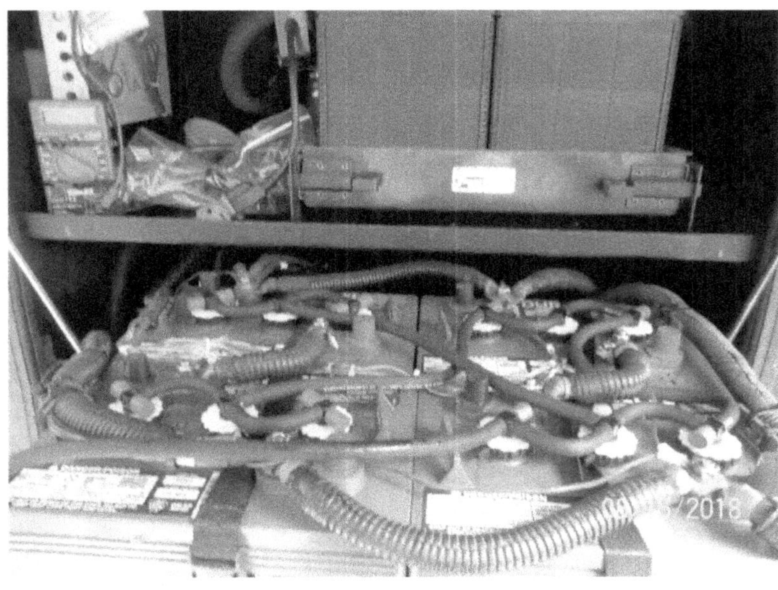

Battery Tender

As winter approaches I read many forum threads asking "should I remove my batteries for the winter and if no, how should I care for them". I have found that if the batteries are in good shape and have proper water levels covering the plates, they will do just fine left in the RV. The one stipulation is you must have a battery tender of some type. If the batteries are kept charged they will not freeze and will be in good shape in the spring.

I have used two battery tenders, one for each battery bank for the past ten years and have had no problems. One tender I connected to my coach bank of four 6 volt batteries and one I connected to my chassis bank of two 12 volt batteries. A plus with the tenders I use is they can be left connected through the summer months when you are

using the RV and they do not interfere with your on board battery charger. All I do in the fall is turn off the battery disconnect switches and plug them in. They are a no muss no fuss solution.

I have gotten my tenders from Harbor Freight. They are usually on sale in the fall for $19.98. This is a great price for a battery charger/tender. The tenders come with a bracket that allows them to easily be attached to the battery tray.

You can fine them here:

https://www.harborfreight.com/15-amp-three-stage-onboard-battery-charger-maintainer-99857.html

1.5 Amp Three Stage Onboard 12V Battery Charger/Maintainer

CEN-TECH.

Cen-Tech® - Item#99857

Recharge batteries up to three times faster than conventional units with this three-stage, fully

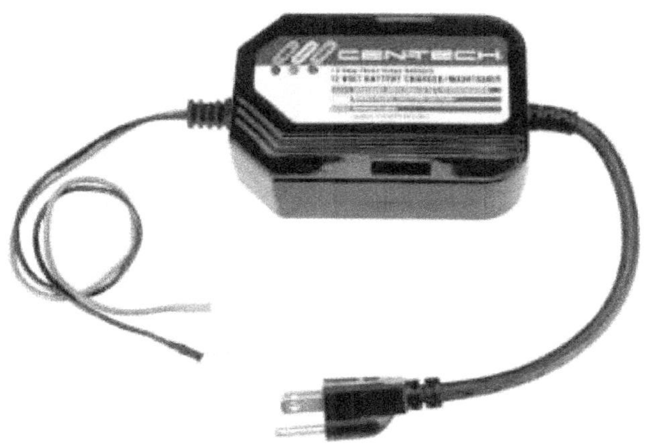

automatic battery charger. This high frequency battery charger uses the latest technology to prolong battery life and is great for maintaining batteries while in storage. The battery charger is equipped with overload protection, short circuit protection and reverse polarity protection for added safety. LED charge indicators let you know when your battery is charged

Charge or maintain 12 volt batteries or 6 volt batteries connected in series

Three-stage fully automatic charge controller protects and prolongs battery life

Automatically switches to trickle charging to prevent overcharging

Bracket for permanent mounting in battery bay

LED charge indicators show status at a glance

RV Tire Safety

I am by no means a tire expert so if you see something you believe is in error or need additional information I urge you to speak to a professional in your tire shop.

RV tires are probably one of the most missunderstood and abused items on your RV. Proper care can give you many years of safe and reliable service from your tires. Improper care can be dangerous.

Do you know that most tire manufactures say to replace RV tires every five to ten years? I give this spread because depending on the manufacture it may be only five years while other manufactures say seven years and a few stretch it to ten years. The age of your tire can easily be determined by reading the DOT code stamped onto the tire. When I say easily I may be taking liberties because the DOT code is usually stamped on the inside of the tire thus requiring you to crawl under the RV. Please be careful when doing this. Never go under a motorhome raised on its jack system, make sure the RV

is properly blocked and take a flashlight. You will be looking for a stamp as is shown in the picture to the right. The information of interest is the Manufacture Date code. In this picture the code "4708". This means the tire was made the

47th week of 2008. Not only should you know the age of your existing tires but when buying new tires make sure the dealer is not selling you some that have been in the back of the warehouse for several years and are already half way through their useful life.

Next is tire inflation. Running an under inflated tire places excessive stress on the tire side wall due to the constant flexing that occurs and can result in a tire blow out. Over inflation can cause the tire to crown, only the center of the tire hits the surface of the road. This results in poor traction, poor breaking, and a rough ride. Every manufacture of RV tires recommends that the tire be inflated according to the weight of the RV. If you go on line you can find a table similar to the one shown for your specific tire. This chart is for a 275/80R22.5 LRG tire. The RV in question is a motor home. The front axle was found to be carying 11020 pounds when weighed which equals 5510 pounds per tire. Therefore by the chart the tire should be inflated to 95 PSI. The rear tires are duals and that axle was found to be carrying 18760 pounds or 9380 pounds per pair. Therefore by the chart the rear tires should be inflated to 85 psi. Choose the closest larger value to your weight.

275/80R22.5 LRG

PSI		70	75	80	85	90	95	100	105	110
kPa		480	520	550	590	620	660	690	720	760
LBS	SINGLE	4500	4725	4940	5155	5370	5510	5780	5980	6175
	DUAL	8190	8600	9080	9380	9770	10140	10520	10880	11350
KG	SINGLE	2040	2140	2240	2340	2440	2500	2620	2710	2800
	DUAL	3720	3900	4120	4260	4440	4600	4780	4940	5150

If you are

unable to weigh the RV you can always use the GAWR (Gross Axle Weight Rating) found on the RV weight sticker but actual loaded weight is the better way to go. Your tire pressure should be checked at least every two weeks and only when the tire is cold. I check mine every trip using a TPMS (Tire Pressure Monitor System). These are great tools and you may wish to look into one.

OK, we know the tire age and the correct PSI to put into the tire. Now we need to perform a simple tire inspection. This is done by rubbing your hand over the tire. You are looking for any scalloping or cupping that is a sign of improper tire wear. If you find this consult a professional to determine the cause and fix. You also want to inspect the side wall both inside wall and outside wall for any bulges. If you find one do not run any further on that tire as you will risk a blow out. Have the tire replaced ASAP.

I bet you did not think I could go on so long about tires. Well I am not done yet. Off to the campground we go and what is the first

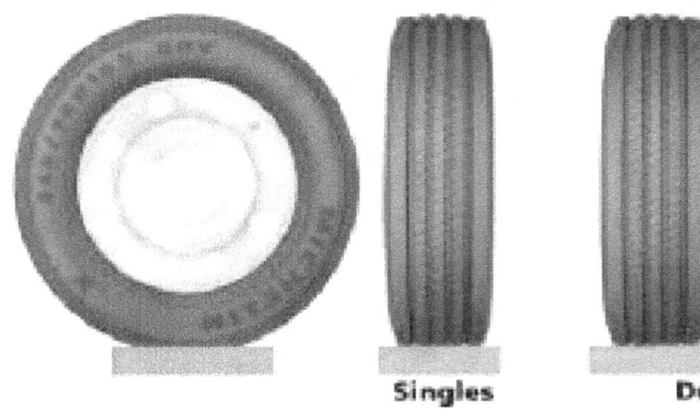

Examples of Proper Tire Blocking

thing we do? Level the RV. There is a right way and wrong way to do this so as to not damage your tires. If done wrong you could cause internal steel belt separation and/or side wall failure. The two diagrams show you everything you need to know on this topic. Please follow them.

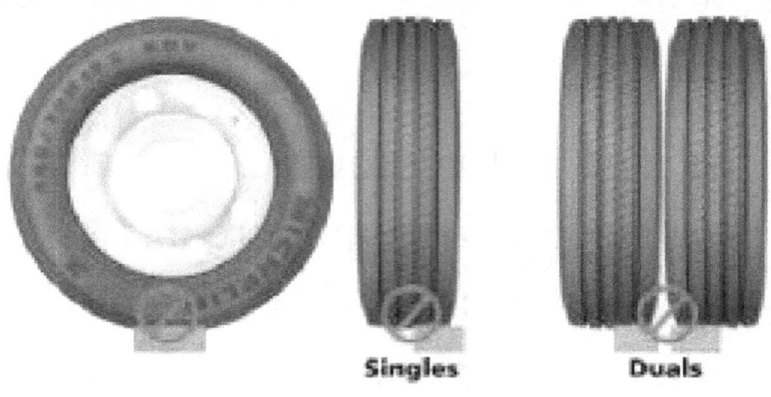

Example of Incorrect Tire Blocking

Last topic is tire care once you return home. RV tires are different than automobile tires as the manufacturer knows the tire will be sitting most of the time. To protect the tire they put more of an oil into the rubber blend. To care for your tire only wash it with a mild soap and water so this oil remains on the tire. It is also a

good idea to cover the tire to keep direct sunlight from causing premature aging. RV dealers sell tire covers for this purpose. I have a set I use in the winter months but in the summer I use windshield sun screens. I find them easier to install and they fold up into a small compact bundle for taking with.

Secrets of FreightLiner's LBCU

The Light Bare Control Unit (LBCU) first appeared in the summer of 2006. As the reader you might be wondering why I have included this topic with maintenance. The reason is the LBCU is loaded with features that will help you maintain your coach and diagnosis faults.

In the maintenance menus you can set reminders to perform critical maintenance functions. These reminders will be displayed in the favorites section when they come due.

In the diagnostics menus you can pull the trouble codes from any of the on board systems, test the dash gauges, and test the LBCU warning lights. You even have the ability to monitor all the sensors on the Freightliner chassis and set them to aid in troubleshooting problems.

If you have not I urge you to become acquainted with the many functions of the LBCU. To follow I have listed the functions and how to access them.

Selecting and programming the SETUP; MAINTENANCE; DIAGNOSTICS display

1. Turn in the ignition switch but do not crank the engine.
2. Wait until the Favorite Display is shown on the Light Bar

   Control Unit (LBCU). You may have to toggle the dash
   mounted joy stick/toggle stick left to achieve this display.
3. Using the dash mount joy stick toggle to the right and hold
   until the following display is presented.   This display
   shows three options.

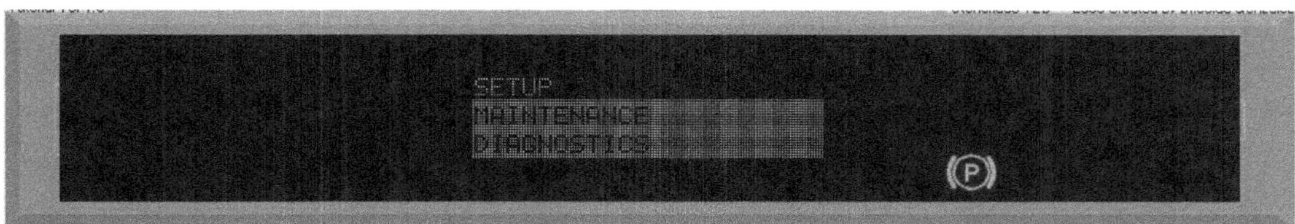

4. Using the joy stick toggle down to select the category of
   interest then toggle right to make changes

5. SETUP Category, option
   Set time and date
   Configuration Checklist
   Select Metric/English
   Set Display Properties

6. Maintenance (used to set up reminder intervals)
        Engine Oil
        Engine Air Filter
        Engine Fuel Filter
        Generator Oil
        Generator Fuel Filter
        Transmission Oil

7. Diagnostics (used to test and trouble shoot engine and drive train problems)
        Check Gauges
        Check Icons
        Check Inputs
        Check Outputs
        Engine Diagnostics
        Coolant System Diag
        ABS Diagnostice
        Hardware/Software Ver
        Check Internal Data
        Odometer Diagnostics
        Input Override

Selecting and saving the information shown on the Favorite Display

1. Turn on the ignition switch but do not crank the engine.
2. Wait until the Favorite Display is shown on the Light Bar Control Unit (LBCU). You may have to toggle the dash

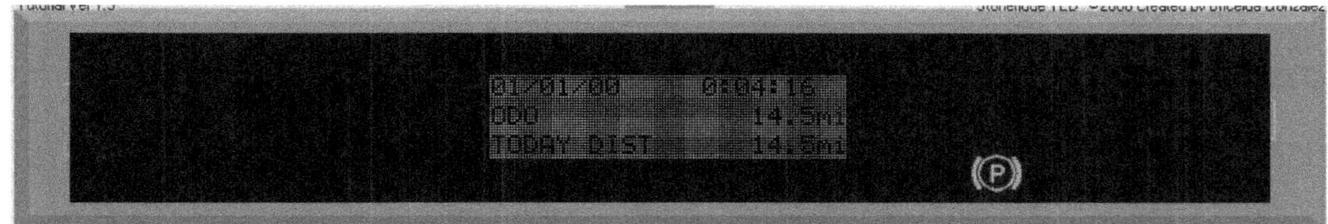

   mounted joy stick/toggle stick left to achieve this display.

3. Using the dash mount joy stick, toggle switch down toggle to select the row to be setup.   Toggle once to highlight the first row, twice to highlight the second row. There are a total of eight unique rows that may be highlighted.

4. After selecting the desired row to setup (it must be highlighted) toggle and hold the joy stick to the right until the format options "Category Select List" is displayed.

5. Toggle down to selection the option for this row.

6. Right toggle then release the joy stick to select this option. Once completed if the row is highlighted you can then

right toggle the joy stick to display sub category options. Read next section for these.

7. Wait for the highlight to disappear.

8. If desired you may setup the remaining seven rows by repeating steps 4 to 7. Note: the Favorite display will only show three rows at a time but there are a total of eight rows that may be setup. Think of the display as a rotary cylinder showing only three selections at a time like the cylinder of a slot machine.

9. Turn off the ignition switch. The changes will be saved and available the next time you start the coach.

Favorite Display Options

1. Date & Time   month/day/year hour:minute:second
             month/day hour:minute:second
             hour:minute:second

2. Odometer

3. Compass; Outside Temperature (this feature is not implemented on many coaches)

4. Today's distance; Today's time; Today's Fuel; Today's fuel economy; Today's average speed; Today's idle time

5. Leg distance; Leg time; Leg Fuel; Leg fuel economy; Leg average speed; Leg Idle time

6. Trip distance; Trip time; Trip Fuel; Trip fuel economy; Trip average speed; Trip Idle time

7. Road speed; Cruise speed; Engine RPM; Oil Pressure: Instantaneous fuel economy; Fuel used; Engine hours; Engine temperature; Turbo pressure; Voltage

8. Transmission temperature; Transmission gear

9. Generator hours (this feature is not implemented on all coaches)

Mini Blade Fuse Circuit Breaker

You have just had a fuse
blow. You replace it and the
fuse blows again. Now
comes the job of determining
where a short circuit or an
over load exists. You begin
tracing out the circuit, believe
you have found the problem
and pop in another fuse. It
blows again. The dilemma is
you only have a finite number of fuses to play this game with.
The solution could be a manual reset fuse type circuit breaker
with the following features:

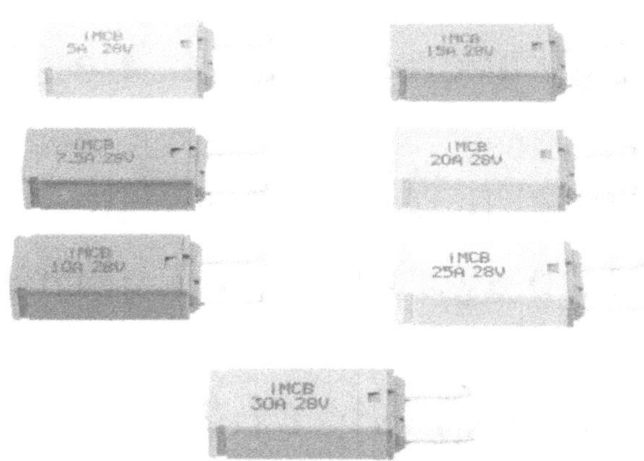

- Will fit in place of standard ATM fuses
- Has over-current protection
- Material: Plastic+Metal
- Size: Approx 1.4*0.5*0.2 Inch

A complete set from 5 amp to 30 amp can be had for around
$27.00 at this location

Another useful tool would be a device that can measure the voltage and current draw in the bad circuit. There are several such devices on the market made for this. One, manufactured by CEN-TEC is their "30 Amp Automotive

Fuse Circuit Tester". It is cost effective and easy to use. Its test leads plug directly into the ATC blade-style fuse slots. The unit reads voltage and current, has an auto shut off after 30 seconds of non-use, a 12 volt Test range, and 0-30 amps resolution

Cost for this tool is under $20.00. One can be found here

https://www.amazon.com/Amp-Automotive-Fuse-Circuit-Tester/dp/B004ZUJNB8/ref=sr_1_4?ie=UTF8&qid=15169766 49&sr=8-4&keywords=30+Amp+Automotive+Fuse+Circuit+Tester

Repair Fogged RV Windows

Have you notice that the dual-pane windows on your RV have started to fog? What has occurred is after years of rolling down the road the shaking and rattling of the RV has caused the seal between the two panes of glass to fail. At first the fog may be light and not a big issue but left untreated the windows will eventually become opaque and impossible to see through. This situation can be especially dangerous in a motorhome, as it could impair your ability to see while driving!

This happen to me a few years back so while at a FMCA rally I paid to have one of my windows defogged and in the process learned how to do it myself.

- The tools required are
- Number 2 square head screw driver
- Flat blade screw driver
- 000 Steel wool
- Packing knife with extra blades
- Flat razor blade scraper with extra blades
- Window cleaning materials
- Second Skin Damplifier Butyl Rope (3/8" X 15' Each)
- Butyl Tape 1/8" x 1" x 50' Black

First step in the repair is to identify the bad window and remove it from the RV. For this you will need a number 2 square head screw driver. On the inside of the RV remove the screws from the window mounting ring then gently push the window out from the bottom. It is good to have two people for this operation, one inside the RV and one outside. The window will often have caulk along the top edge and may offer resistance to the removal process.

As seen to the right in this example there is no mistaken that this window needs help. Once removed inspect the window frame. You will find that several screws hold the frame together. Removing  these will allow the glass to be removed. You will be left with just the window glass

.

Next the window glass will need to be separated. If the portion you are working on has the slide handle attached remove it by running the packing knife along and down its 

edge on both sides. This is to break the caulk seal. Then with a screw driver gently pry the aluminum slider off. Be careful here not to break the glass.

Once the slider is removed separate the two panes of glass. This is accomplished by inserting the packing knife between the pains and cutting the seal. You will find that

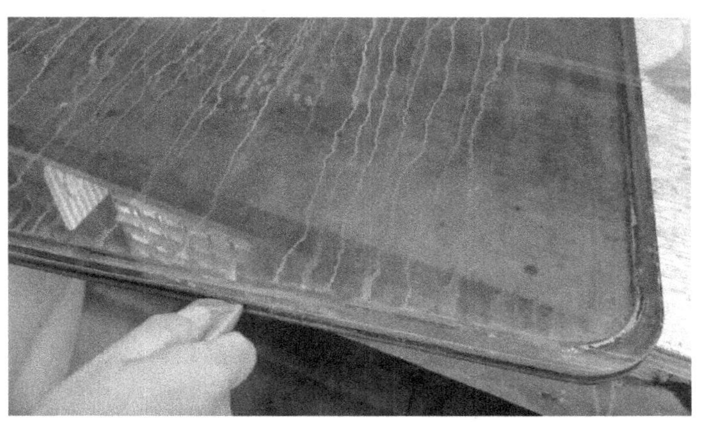

this is easy as a rubber or silicone material has been used to seal the panes together and in most cases has separated from the glass, thus the reason for the failure. Again be careful not to break the glass.

Once separated clean all four sides of the glass. You will want them spotless. This is where the flat razor blade and 000 steel wool will come in. If the fogging has gone on for several years the interior glass may be etched beyond the point of normal cleaning or polishing and will need to be replaced. What some people have done here is to purchase a piece of Plexiglas for the interior portion of the window rather than finding a shop that can cut tempered glass.

Now the hard work is complete. All that is left is assembly and reinsertion into the RV. Run a bead of the Second Skin Damplifier Butyl Rope (3/8" X 15' Each) around the edge of one piece of glass then press the second piece of glass on top making a sandwich. Do not press too hard on the sandwich as the overall thickness of the window needs to be a tight fit in the window frame seal. It is better to do small adjustments when fitting to the frame. Put the newly cleaned and assembled double pane of glass back in the window frame. If a pull bar needs to go on attach it with a bead of clear silicone and press over the glass.

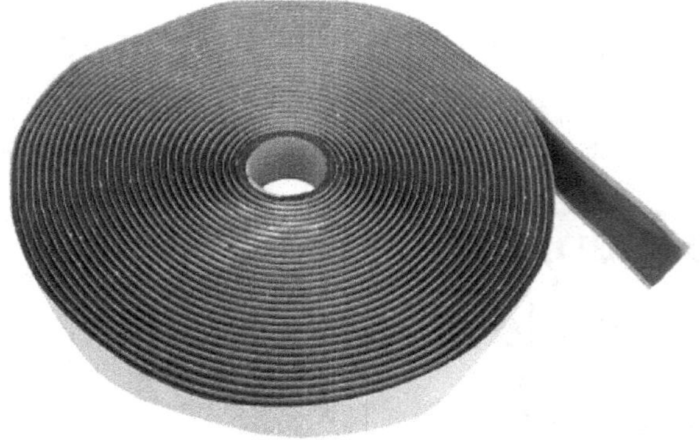

Run a strip of Butyl Tape 1/8" x 1" around the window frame to insure a water tight seal and reinstall in the RV.

If you work right along you can repair one window in less than two hours.

The Butyl material is available on amazing.com. Cost is about $20.00 for both rolls. I always keep some handy in the tool box.

RV Roof Maintenance

The most important part of every RV as well as the most neglected is the RV roof. A good roof and you have a good RV. A damaged or leaking roof and you can get spots on the ceiling, ceiling separation, mold, and possibly RV delamination. All of these issues can ruin your RV fun. A simple way to prevent any of this is periodic roof inspection and repair of any issue that is found.

There are three types of roofing used on RVs. Fiberglass, EPDM (Ethylene Propylene Diene Monomer), and TPO (Thermal Poly Olefin). The latter two are a type of rubber roof system and have a life span of no more than ten years. Fiberglass roofs are more low maintenance than rubber roofs, will last longer and by many owners are more preferable than the rubber roofs.

My RV has a fiberglass roof. At least once a year, normally in the fall, I wash it and then inspect it and all the seals for cracking. Any issues I find I repair. The two products I prefer are Dicor to repair the seal cracks and EternaBond tape to repair any damage to the fiberglass. The EternaBond comes in black and white to match the RV. Dicor is normally white. I like the Dicor self leveling lap seal. If you apply Dicor in the fall do not wait too long as Dicor takes longer to dry in cool weather. While these products are expensive they are the best out there and the roof is one area where scrimping can get you in trouble.

EPDM and TPO roofs can be maintenance the same as fiberglass with the exception that you should wash them only with products recommended for the specific roof material. I like Dicor rubber roof cleaner. Another product I have heard

professional RV repair shops sometimes use is Wisk laundry detergent.

Let's say that your rubber roof is nearing the end of its useful life but has no tairs in it and is not brittle. This recently happen to a friend of mine. This was his solution in his words.

Obtained the appropriate materials

- Hengs Roof coat rubber roof treatment
- Dicor sealant used to repair cracked and dried seals and around appliances and vents/
- Eternabond tape used to fix roof edging, and roof cracks.
- Tide for a good roof cleaning.
- Cleaning brush, paint roller, paint brushes
- Ladders and platforms to allow easy access to the RV roof.

Temporarily remove items on the roof like solar panels and vent covers, then scrub roof down with Tide and rinse. I purchased two gallons of the Hengs Roof Care to cover square feet. The plan is to apply two thin coats.

There was a need to make some repairs to the edges of the rubber (I followed an example I found on YouTube and used EternaBond tape. With the second coat done I used about 1 1/2 gallons of sealer.

Once the roof coating cured I reinstall the solar panels sealing the mounting brackets using dicor.   I plan to use the remaining 1/2 gallon on another coat around the edges and seals; I'll just wait a couple more days.

To follow are pictures of before and after. You can see the difference and the roof is good for several more years.

Marine Tex Super Epoxy

A good friend Mike Jones turned me on to the benefits of Marine Tex. He did a super job on a write up and said I could reprint it.

I wanted to let everyone know about an amazing substance known as Marine Tex. I've found that most RV'ers I have talked to have never heard of it. It's marketed more to the boating world. This stuff is truly incredible. It's a 2 part epoxy glue/putty that has approximately the consistency of toothpaste. I have fixed thousands things with this stuff. It's expensive but If I look at the number of things I have fixed with it that I thought I would have to replace, it is the most frugal product you can possibly buy.

When you have something made of plastic or metal that is hopelessly broken Mix up some Marine Tex. Smear on a blob and piece it back together. You can shape it like putty and use it to replace pieces if some are missing. Once it's dry you can sand it, file it, grind it, drill it and even thread it. I have had bolt holes that have stripped out. I fill them with Marine Tex.

Drill it. Re-thread it. Put in a new bolt, and it has held for years. I used to have a little racing boat with a 500 horsepower V8 engine. It developed a stress crack in the engine block. A welder said it couldn't be welded, so I smeared on a big blob of Marine Tex and it held for years. Twice now, the refrigerator door in my motorhome has swung open while driving, and snapped one of the plastic hinges. Both times, I have reconstructed the hinge with big blob of Marine Tex. It has held for years. A friend of mine recently bought an old motorhome that had not been winterized. It had a big crack in the water heater tank. I smeared a big blob of Marine Tex on it and so far it's holding fine.

These photos are of one of my refrigerator door shelves that broke. I used Marine Tex to put it back together. The repair may look sloppy, but it's strong.

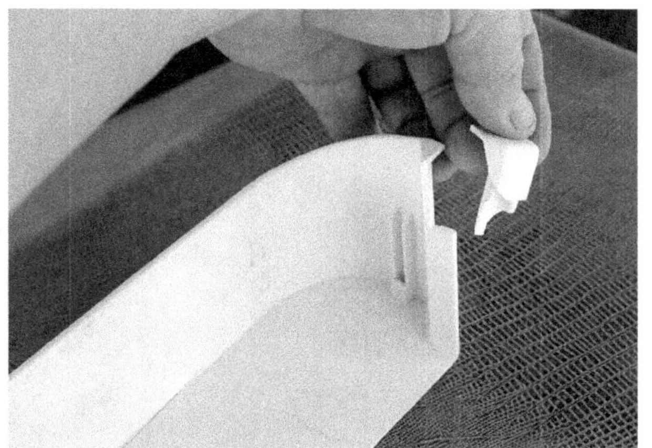

For anyone that has used Bondo. This stuff feels very much like working with Bondo, only it's about a million times stronger, and adheres about a million times better. Being epoxy based, it also dries more flexible, so it doesn't crack and flake off like Bondo does. On metal, it's nearly as strong as a weld. On plastic, it's about 10 times stronger than the plastic itself.

It's available in white and gray. Get the gray. It's MUCH stronger. The gray has actual flakes of metal in it to make it stronger. You can find it in boating stores, or Search Amazon. Prices start at $15.00 for a 2 ounce package. I get the 12 ounce can. Costs about $40, and has lasted me about 10 years now.

Emergency Supplies

What emergency supplies do you carry in your RV? Here is my list and the reason for each item.

- Oil Valvoline Premiun Blue SAE 15W40 rating CES20081 or CJ-4/LS in the event I need to top off. I do not like to mix oil types and this insures I have what is in the coach.
- Oil Mobil DelVac SynTrans MBL 98Hx54 for the Transmission. This is the new synthetic oil introduced back in 2008. I have never looked to see how easy it is to get and I have it.
- Oil Valvoline Gear Oil 80W90 Rating L-2105-D GL-5 to be used for wheel bearings in the event of a wheel seal failure to get me to a shop.
- One gallon FleetCharge antifreeze in the event I need to top off. If the antifreeze is low the coach will go into limp mode.
- Spare set of windshield wiper blades. They are not available everywhere if needed.
- One un-mounted spare tire. There are many places in the US that you cannot get a matching motorhome

tire if you have a flat. You could be stranded for over a week.

- Power Service Diesel Kleen + Cetane Boost fuel additive. Keeps the injectors clean and increases fuel millage by 1 mpg when towing my toad. I put it in at every fill up.
- Dayco 5080925 Poly Rib Serpentine Belt. This fits my Cummins 6.7 liter ISB engine. I have had to use this more than once.
- Marine Tex Epoxy Putty. Great for making many kinds of repairs.
- Spray silicone. To lubricate slides, tow bar, and other things requiring a grease less lube.
- PB Blaster spray lubricant for things like door locks and latches.
- An assortment of tie wraps.
- One roll of Gorilla tape.
- Eternabond tape to make emergency repairs.
- Assorted sizes of hardware from Harbor Freight and Square Bit driver

STOREHOUSE
320 PC.
STAINLESS STEEL
SCREW ASSORTMENT
ITEM 67679
A full selection of stainless steel sheet metal screws in one convenient kit!
Stainless steel resists rust and corrosion
Self-threading is ideal for use in sheet metal with pilot hole
Includes flat head, oval head and pan head screws with Phillips drive
Neatly organized in a divided PVC storage case with chart inside box lid for easy selection
320 Piece Set Includes

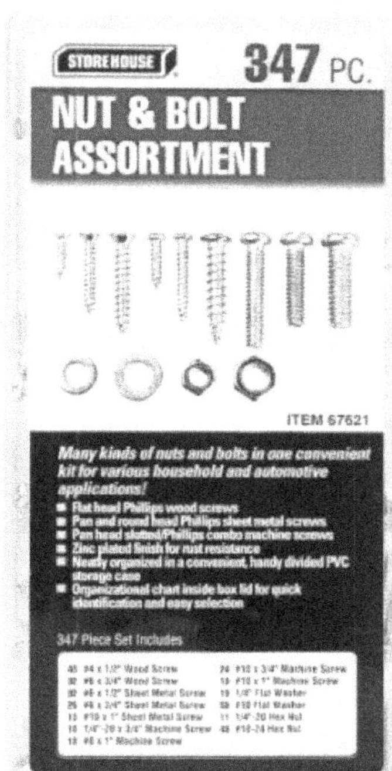
STOREHOUSE
347 PC.
NUT & BOLT
ASSORTMENT
ITEM 67621
Many kinds of nuts and bolts in one convenient kit for various household and automotive applications!
Flat head Phillips wood screws
Pan and round head Phillips sheet metal screws
Pan head slotted/Phillips combo machine screws
Zinc plated finish for rust resistance
Neatly organized in a convenient, handy divided PVC storage case
Organizational chart inside box lid for quick identification and easy selection
347 Piece Set Includes

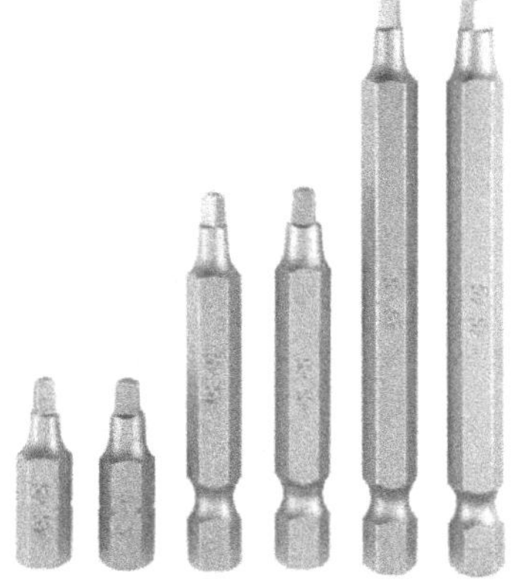

POSTSCRIPT

I hope you found the information helpful. Thank you for reading it.

James Edward Clicquennoi